Battle
Book

Transportal

Tops/Ups

Drops/Lifts

Downs/Grounds

Signatures/Burns

Freezes

Powermoves

Battle Notes

Extra Bboy Sh*t

TRANSPORTAL

Travelling Moves & Concepts.
Entering the Cipher, Exiting the Cipher,
& Monotony Breaker-Uppers.

TOPS & UPS

Poses, Toprocks, & Uprocks.
All Upright Moves and Concepts.
This Level can include Knees.

DROPS & LIFTS

Also called "Go Downs" & "Come Ups."
Fresh ways to go down to the ground
and come back up.

Note:
In general with exceptions,
once you go down,
stay down.

DOWNROCKS

Also called "Bottom Rock" & "Floor Rock."
All Moves and Concepts are at Floor Levels.

SIGNATURES & BURNS

Signatures are special unique concepts that you invented or are known for.

Burns are concepts that clown your opponent, taunting and dissing them typically in a comedic or showy way. Not usually intended to be taken personally, ...but whatever.

FREEZES

A "Freeze" is both a noun and a verb. The *Baby Freeze* is a name for a ground position. Freezing is an action of coming to a hault from movement.

Note:
Freezes are poses at Down/Ground level. Poses are freezes at Up/Top levels. ...kinda.

<u>POWERMOVES</u>

All moves and concepts containing an explosion. An explosion is a moment of "let-go" when your momentum takes over.

Explosions can be a One-off: like a Flip,
Sustained: like a Backspin.
Perpetual: like a Windmill.

BATTLE NOTES

Concepts, Strategies, &
General Notes on Bboy Warfare.

THE BOOK OF POWER
List of Powermoves by Family

HANDSTAND FAMILY

Handstands • Scissors • Hops • 1990's • 2000's
Elbowss • Elbow spins • Variations

HEADSTAND FAMILY

Headstand • Headspin • Stop n go (tapping)
Floats • Drills • Hurricanes • Head slide

WINDMILL FAMILY

Backspin • Windmill • Nasties (Ball Breakers) • Kyriaki
Mills (hopping) • Mummies • HandCuffs. • Icy-Ice
Halo (Traxx) • Air Track (Air Traxx) • Babies
Mudspills • Munchmills • Superman Mills (Bellymills
Chestmills) • Ultramans (arms above the head rolling
across hands; mistakenly referred to as Supermans
by newer generations.) • Variations

SWIPE FAMILY

Swipe • Anchored • Rotating • 1 Leg • 2 Legs
Fore-leg • Hind-leg • Air Flare (No leg Swipe) • Variations

HAND WALKS FAMILY

Turtle (known in the west as a Crabwalk) • Handglide
Air Wolf • Pogo • Jack Hammer • UFO • Monkey walks
Exotic & Variations

LINEAR POWER FAMILY

Kip-ups • Bronco • V-kick (Russian Kick) • Variations

AERIAL FAMILY

Flips • Aerials • Variations • (Air Flares)

FLARE FAMILY

Legs Together/Apart • Anchored • Rotating
Skipping • Leg Variations • Tricks w hands

BBoyAcademy.com
Mouthzilla.com
DrewLooner
@Gmail.com

73760515R00041

Made in the USA
Columbia, SC
06 September 2019